Trigp[illegible] District:

Peter Naldrett

Peter Naldrett is a journalist and geography teacher who spends much of his free time walking with his family in the Peak District National Park. Frustrated by the lack of definitive guides to the area's highest hikes, he set out to capture some of the more challenging routes in his new book, *Trigpoint Walks In The Peak District: The Dark Peak*. He previous book, *Poems About Places*, details his journeys around the world.

After spells working at several newspapers, Peter entered a career in teaching and currently works at a South Yorkshire secondary school. He also writes regularly as a freelance writer, contributing a weekly music column to the *Manx Independent* and a wide range of features to national magazines. His writing credits include *The Daily Telegraph, The Big Issue, Classic Rock, Geographical* and *Dogs Monthly*.

Peter lives close to the Peak District with his wife, Nicola, and son, Toby.

www.peter-naldrett.co.uk

Also by Peter Naldrett:

Poems About Places

"A journey around the world in poems"

Dean Pepall, BBC Radio Sheffield

"*Poems About Places* charts Peter's journeys around the world"

Isle of Man Newspapers

"A series of thought-provoking and insightful poems"

Terry Ellis, Rotherham Advertiser

For Nicola

Trigpoint Walks In The Peak District
The Dark Peak

Peter Naldrett

First published in the United Kingdom by

Precious Pumpkin Books, 2006.

This revised edition published in the United Kingdom 2006 by Exposure Publishing

An imprint of Diggory Press, Three Rivers, Minions, Liskeard, PL14 5LE

ISBN 1846854377 (978-1-84685-437-8)

Further copies of this book can be bought at

www.peter-naldrett.co.uk

A CIP record of this book is available from the British Library.

First printed 2006

Written and edited by Peter Naldrett

Front and back cover designed by Neil Holt: www.nhphotography.co.uk

Disclaimer: The information in this book is given in good faith and is believed to be correct at the time of publication. Neither the author or the publisher accepts any responsibility for errors or omissions, or for any loss or injury howsoever caused. You alone can judge your own fitness, competence and experience and you should do so before setting out. Walking in the Peak District can be a dangerous activity and only you can judge of level of your own fitness and which walks are suitable for you. Proper equipment and suitable appropriate precautions should always be taken. Do not solely rely on sketch maps for navigation. We strongly recommend the use of appropriate Ordnance Survey maps and a GPS. It is the responsibility of individuals undertaking outdoor activities to approach the activity with caution and, especially if inexperienced, to do so under supervision. The activities described in this book are strenuous and individuals should ensure they are suitably fit and correctly dressed before embarking upon them.

The walks

The aim of this book

It has been a frustration of mine for some time that I could not find a book which brought together all the highest peaks in the Peak District for people who loved to walk and relished a challenge. This book has been written to bring those peaks together in one place and describe the challenge that I set myself: to climb the highest peaks in the Dark Peak. The walks I have described are obviously not the only routes to the trigpoints, and numerous other paths can be found by consulting Ordnance Survey maps. This book, then, should always be used in conjunction with the relevant maps that are recommended within the walk descriptions – both to get the most out of the surrounding area and help you plan your chosen route without getting lost. My aim is for this book to provide a comprehensive guide to the highest peaks and trigpoints that are accessible to the public in the northern areas of the Peak District. I have described the routes that I took to achieve the goal of "bagging" all the trigpoints and provide these destinations in list form for you to plan your own visits.

It was in 2004 when I spawned the idea of a walking book detailing routes to the trigpoints in the Peak District. The book you have bought focuses specifically on the area of the northern Peak District, known because of the dark gritstone found there as The Dark Peak. The area of the Peak District found to the south is limestone country known as The White Peak and a specialised book on trigpoint walks in this area will follow the release of this book.

Why trigpoints?

These curious looking four foot tall concrete pillars are found the length and breadth of the country – so why should they be the focus of our walks? Well, the simple answer is that they are to be found atop the highest peaks in the area so reaching them should provide walkers with their greatest challenge and reward them with fantastic views. But beyond the recreational enjoyment we get out of them today, the trigpoints we incorporate into our walks had a very important role in days gone by.

Trigpoints were assembled in the 1930s by Ordnance Survey, who used them to chart the shape and height of the country so they could produce the maps we all rely on today. It was a massive undertaking and there are over 6,200 pillars placed in key parts of the country – all a testimony to the incredible mapping operation that took place. Each trigpoint has a metal disc inserted into the top which can support a theodolite (a type of compass built into a telescope) and enable the surveyors to accurately record the topography of the surrounding area. Each trigpoint was put into an accurately measured position, which enabled cartographers to survey everything in sight in relation to the other trigpoints that can be seen from there. The process of this was called "triangulation" and this gives a clue to the origin of the name trig points. The heroic attempt to map the country in

this way has led to the excellent Ordnance Survey maps that we can all use today, as well as the concept of the "national grid" so we can give accurate co-ordinates. I have used many of these co-ordinates in this book and it is essential that you become familiar with how to read maps and use grid references.

In modern times, trigpoints mainly have a recreational use and they are often the goal for walkers as they stride to the top of hills and mountains. How many of us have taken a photo next to a trigpoint, touched one with exhausted pride or even had a packed lunch beside one? But not all trigpoints are on publicly accessible land so you can't just wander up to any of them. What this book tries to do is assemble in one place all the trigs in the Dark Peak which can safely be reached – or at least seen – by walkers.

Unfortunately, many trigpoints have fallen into disrepair over the years and they are often found missing their metal plaques or the triangular

fixing on the top of the trig that was used to screw in the apparatus of the land surveyors. Other trigs have been vandalised and very few are maintained in a way that keeps them in a pristine white condition. Indeed, some of them have disappeared from the landscape entirely, some removed for housing developments and others mindlessly destroyed. The trigpoints described in this book, though, are largely in good shape and respected by the majority of those who visit them – I would urge you to respect them also.

Not all Trigpoints found in Britain today are only of historical value. Some are still used to maintain the accuracy of the GPS (Global Positioning Systems) network and are very much relevant to walkers who use GPS and those who drive in cars with satellite navigation capabilities.

In 2004 I set myself the challenge of walking to the top of every trigpoint in the Dark Peak. This book is a description of my chosen routes.

The routes and maps

The written routes and hand-drawn maps found in this book provide a rough description of my chosen routes but they should not be relied upon for guiding you on a walk. Walkers setting out in the Peak District should do so in conjunction with Ordnance Survey professional maps and make sure they know how to use them beforehand. I have tried to be as accurate as possible with my descriptions, but you should always check your progress on an OS map so you are always aware of where you have been and where you are heading. Take precautions to plan your walk carefully and never rely on a walk description alone. I also advise walkers to take a GPS device and be familiar with how to use it so you can check your location on a map. The hand drawn maps in this book are meant to provide an overview of my own journey only and are not detailed enough for you to find your way around the countryside. I have tried to leave a blank space next to most maps and these are designed for you to scribe your own notes or observations if you decide to walk to that trigpoint.

The measurements

All the routes written have been personally walked by myself. A GPS device was taken on each walk to produce data which could help you plan your walks. Therefore, each walk has details on the distance, time and total ascent you can expect to encounter. Although these were calculated using satellite technology, they are not always as reliable as we would like, so again they are only a guide. The time indicated is also how long it took myself to complete the walk—keep in mind that I will be faster than some and slower than others. Grid references were also taken using GPS technology. The difficulty rating of the walk is a personal opinion and not an exact science.

Walking in the Dark Peak

The Peak District is an area of phenomenal natural beauty, but it can also be an extremely cruel environment. Terrible weather conditions are frequent occurrence in the Peak District and I kept myself aware of this and obtained forecasts whenever I set out walking. Keep an eye on the weather by checking on the BBC website and phoning ahead to the local tourist information centres where you are heading to. In the Peak District, many of the paths are uneven and, although improving in many areas, can provide an added danger. Treks across open countryside can also be on uneven ground and can be dangerous. I always wore sturdy walking boots and had access to waterproofs in case the weather became bad. Fog and low cloud can also be a problem, so I carried a map and compass in case visibility was restricted. I also invested in a GPS system and always took it on the walk for safety reasons. Use these to make sure you always know where you are, always know where you are going and can judge the time and distances involved. The maps in this book are devised as a guide only. They are not detailed enough to rely on and should always be used with official Ordnance Survey maps. Another precaution was to take my mobile phone, although service is not available throughout the Peak District. Finally, it is important to maintain high fluid and energy levels so make sure you always set out with a good supply of water and snacks. All of the above is best carried together in a small rucksack which can fasten to your back and be much more convenient than carrying bags in your hand. Shops are available in most Peak District villages and you would be supporting the local area as well as your appetite by shopping there.

Once you have gathered all the right equipment to enjoy a safe walk in the Peak District, make sure you do not push yourself too hard at first. If you are not an experienced walker, do not try something too difficult to start off with. Try a walk along flat terrain and gradually increase the difficulty of the walks you embark upon. And make sure you also allow enough time for your travels – most people walk at a speed of 3km/2 miles an hour, with this slowing down considerably uphill. You will walk faster on smooth surfaces and well laid tracks than on muddy paths and grassy hills.

If you set yourself a walking challenge in the area, you are advised to take all these precautions and treat the Peak District with respect.

Peter Naldrett

Sheffield. September, 2006.

The Dark Peak Trigpoint Checklist

	Walk No	Walk Name	Date Completed
Southern Trigpoint Walks	WALK 1	Brown Knoll	
	WALK 2	Edale Moor	
	WALK 3	The Edge	
	WALK 4	Harry Hut	
	WALK 5	Kinder Low	
	WALK 6	Mam Tor	
	WALK 7	Winhill Pike	
Eastern TrigpointWalks	WALK 8	High Neb	
	WALK 9	Kirk Edge	
	WALK 10	Ox Stones	
	WALK 11	Stannedge Pole	
	WALK 12	Stanage Edge	
Central TrigpointWalks	WALK 13	Back Tor	
	WALK 14	Higher Shelf Stones	
	WALK 15	Margery Hill	
	WALK 16	Outer Edge	
	WALK 17	West End Moor	
Northern TrigpointWalks	WALK 18	West Nab	
	WALK 19	South Nab	
	WALK 20	Holme Moss	

Walk 1: Brown Knoll

A challenging Peak District hill walk

Trig Point	Brown Knoll at 569m/1867ft (SK 083851)	
Map	LR110, EOL1	
Distance	✪✪✪○○	10.1km/6.25miles
Time	✪✪○○	2hrs 15min
Ascent	✪✪○○○	368m/1207ft
Difficulty	✪✪○○○	Mix of farm tracks and boggy paths
Start and Finish	Off-road parking on A625 (SK 091824)	

Route Parking in the lay-by on the A625, I walked along the road up the hill, taking the track on the left signposted to Hayfield. This is a well used and easy to follow farming track that took me through several gates. I stuck to this track as it wound its' way over two small streams, with the distinctive air shaft visible on the hill to the right. This shaft is linked to the Gowburn Tunnel, which this walk goes over.

As I started to descend into the valley I was able to see the train track emerge on the left. This is the main line between Manchester and Sheffield. Follow the footpath into Roych Clough, where the track passes over two streams and begins heading up the steep hill. Heading through several gates, I kept to the main track and ignored the path which joined from the left. The walk soon entered National Trust land at South Head, where I continued to the brow of the hill and took in the views of Kinder Scout.

At the top of the hill, I branched right at the crossroads (SK 062846) and followed the path which runs along the left side of the dry stone wall. Continuing along this path, the walk went over a stile and kept on the left side of the wall. Ignoring the smaller stiles on the fence to the right, I was heading for the brow of the hill where I saw a major path off to the right. The walk takes the stile to the right when it meets this junction at SK 082855.

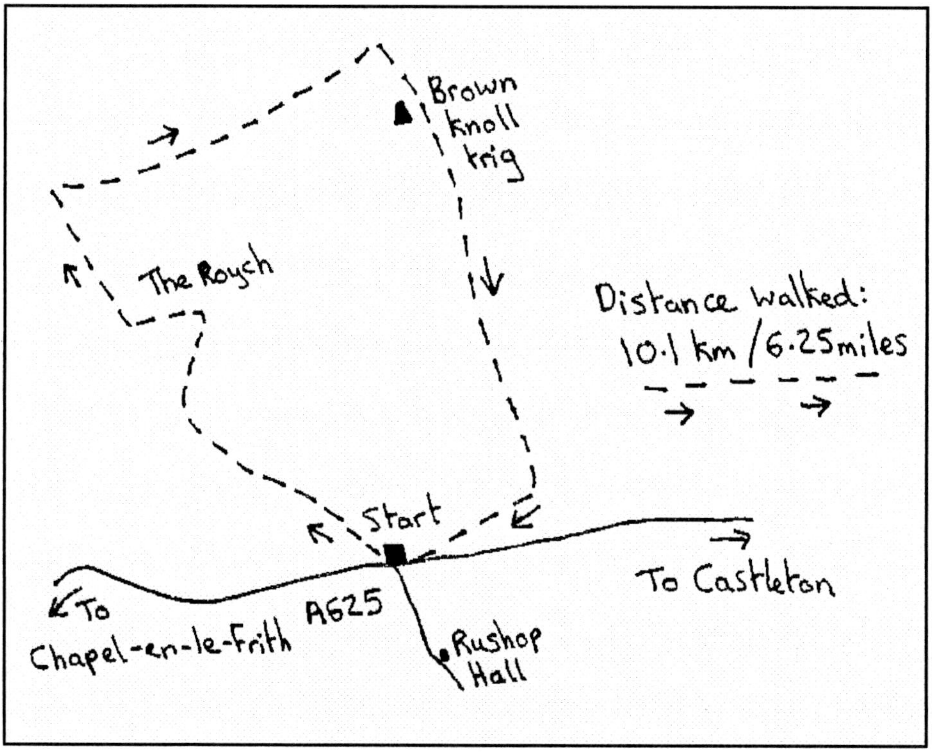

Sticking to the main path, the trigpoint (S2782) came into view on the right. Getting to the trigpoint can pose quite a challenge after heavy rain, when the ground generally becomes really boggy. If the ground is too boggy, do not take risks to reach the trig.

I carried on past the trigpoint, keeping to the path and making sure the air shaft was now on the right. During and after bad weather the path can be difficult to follow so I brought a map and GPS as I followed the path over the peat landscape. The Vale of Edale opened up on your left but I was not heading that way and kept a keen eye out for the path, bearing in mind that it eventually heads to the right of the hill approaching. When I reached a pole marking the path (SK 098831) I turned right and was relieved to notice a great improvement in the quality of the path. Turning right again at the next junction I headed back down to the A625, taking the roadside path back to the start point.

Trigs to spot from the top:

Kinder Low: 2km to the north. **See page 30 of this book.**

The Edge: 4.3km to the north. **See page 22 of this book.**

Mam Tor: 4.7km to the east. **See page 34 of this book.**

Brown Knoll (SK 083851)

The Countryside Code

The countryside is a resource to be enjoyed by walkers. We must do our bit to make sure the countryside continues to be the haven in which we can escape our busy lives. If we abuse it, we threaten to ruin the environment we enjoy. You can do your bit by following The Countryside Code:

1) Be safe. Plan ahead and follow any signs.
2) Leaves gates and property as you find them.
3) Protect plants and animals, and take your litter home.
4) Keep dogs under close control.
5) Consider other people.

Trigpoints on the net

As well as www.trigpointwalks.co.uk, you may like to surf your way to www.trigpointing.co.uk. This website contains an incredible database of all the nation's trigpoints and you can log the ones that you have visited. It really is a trig-baggers dream.

WALK 2 : Edale Moor

A walk up to Kinder Scout, the highest plateau in the Peak District

Trig Point	Edale Moor at 590m/1936ft (SK129878)	
Map	LR110, EOL1	
Distance	✪✪○○○	6.1km/3.8miles
Time	✪✪✪○○	2hr 20min
Ascent	✪✪✪○○	725m/2380ft
Difficulty	✪✪✪✪○	Steep climbs and boggy peat areas
Start and Finish	Track off the A57 at SK 141895	

ROUTE I found this one to be of the most difficult trig walks in the book. It should be approached with respect, with correct clothing, a map and a compass. If the weather looks bad, I would find a nice café instead of tackling this one!

On the A57 to the west of Ladybower Reservoir there is a small track on the southern side of the road that provides parking at the start of this tricky cross-country trek. The track is on the opposite side of the A57 to Hayridge Farm at grid reference (SK 141895). From this start point, I headed through the gate and followed the footpath to open country.

Crossing the River Ashop using the bridge, I then turned left onto a farm track. This path took me past a farm house on the right and over a stream in a small dip before bringing me out at a gate which met another track. I took a right here and went towards the farm house, but before I reached the gate to the house I saw a steep path up to the left, and I made my way up. Near to the top I started to see grouse shooting butts, which can actually provide much needed shelter in bad weather. I soon reached a white-topped pole marker and at this point (SK 143886), turned right and followed the path past other shooting bases. As the grouse butts came to an end, I continued in the same direction along the path that ran to the right of a ruined wall. At grid reference SK 134883 I reached the edge of Edale Moor and found a path running from left to right. I ignored this path and took the route straight ahead. This took me in a south-westerly direction and soon I was able to see Madwoman's Stones in front of me. On a clear day from the stones you can see the trigpoint to the west.

I needed a compass for this section of the walk as I needed to keep

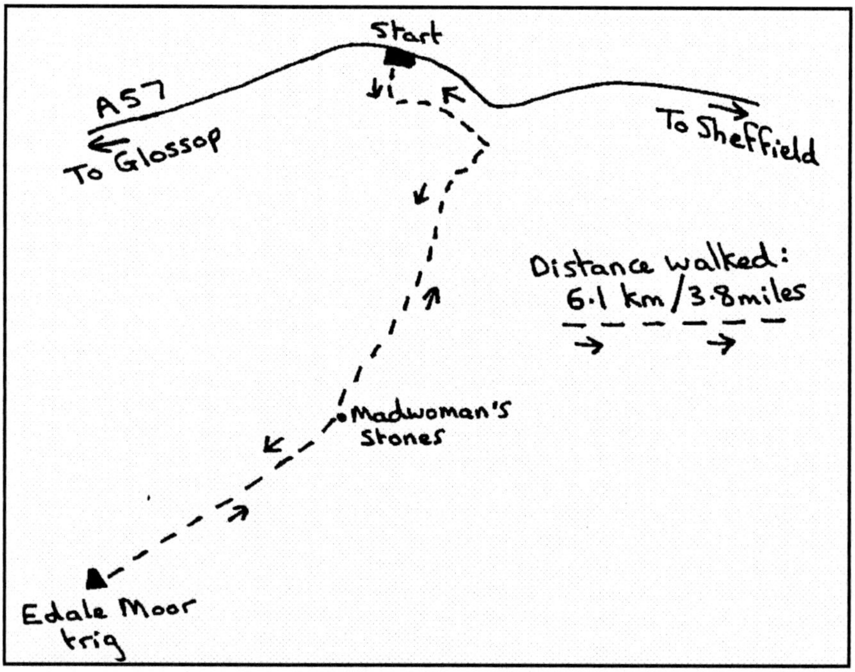

heading in a westerly direction and there is no obvious path to follow across the boggy moorland. The trig (S4231) is often in the middle of an insurmountable peat bog so I had to take real caution here, as with every other section of the walk. I retraced my steps from the trig, first heading east to Madwoman's Stones and from there taking the original path north towards the line of grouse shooting butts. Great care needs to be taken at this stage because other paths lead from Madwoman's Stones and could have taken me a long way off the route. When I reached the white-topped pole at (SK 143886), I turned left and headed back down the grassy bank. At the bottom of the hill, I turned right and then immediately left through a gate, following the path back over the River Ashop to the starting point.

Trigs to spot from the top:

Mam Tor: 4.2km to the south. **See page 34 of this book.**

Kinder Low: 5.1km to the west. **See page 30 of this book.**

Brown Knoll: 5.3km to the south west. **See page 14 of this book.**

The Dark Peak rocks

The Dark Peak is so called because of the distinctive shadowy shades of the local stone found in the area. A far cry from the light limestone colours of The White Peak, the natural stone of The Dark Peak is gritstone and shale.

The origins of the stone in this part of The Peak District can be traced back to over 300 million years ago when the land around Castleton and Edale looked extremely different. In fact, the scene that would have met your eyes back then would have looked more like a massive river delta like that found at the mouth of the Mississippi. In the northern Peak District at that time a huge river was flowing into a warm tropical sea and bringing with it mud and sand from large mountain ranges to the north. The sediment that was being transported towards the sea by the river fell to the bottom of the river bed and gradually started to build up in alternating layers of sand and mud. Over millions of years the sediment was compacted and the huge pressure turned it into a hard rock, with the sand becoming gritstone and the mud turning into shale.

The landscape that you see around you as you walk in the Dark Peak is more than just visually stimulating. By looking at the rocks you are walking past, you can get an insight into what this part of Britain was like in an age long before the dinosaurs.

Of course, we should treasure the glorious rocks that are to be found in the Peak District. Do not take any samples with you as you explore the area and respect it at all times.

WALK 3: The Edge

Another steep climb up Kinder on popular paths

Trig Point	The Edge at 624m/2047ft (SK 076893)	
Map	LR110, EOL1	
Distance	✪✪✪✪☆	13km/8.1miles
Time	✪✪✪☆☆	2hr 55min
Ascent	✪✪✪✪✪	1001m/3285ft
Difficulty	✪✪✪✪☆	Steep climbs on well used paths
Start and Finish	Off-road parking along the A57 (SK 088929)	

ROUTE Popular off-road parking spaces at the top of the Snake Pass form the starting point for this walk up to the highest plateau in the Peak District.

There are three trig points on Kinder Scout, and oddly enough none of them mark the highest point of 636m above sea level. They do, however, provide three varied routes to the top of this Peak District gem. It should go without saying that Kinder has a reputation as a place where the weather can deteriorate very quickly and where the terrain can become disorientating. Trips to the top should only be made with a map, compass and GPS, if possible, to keep you company.

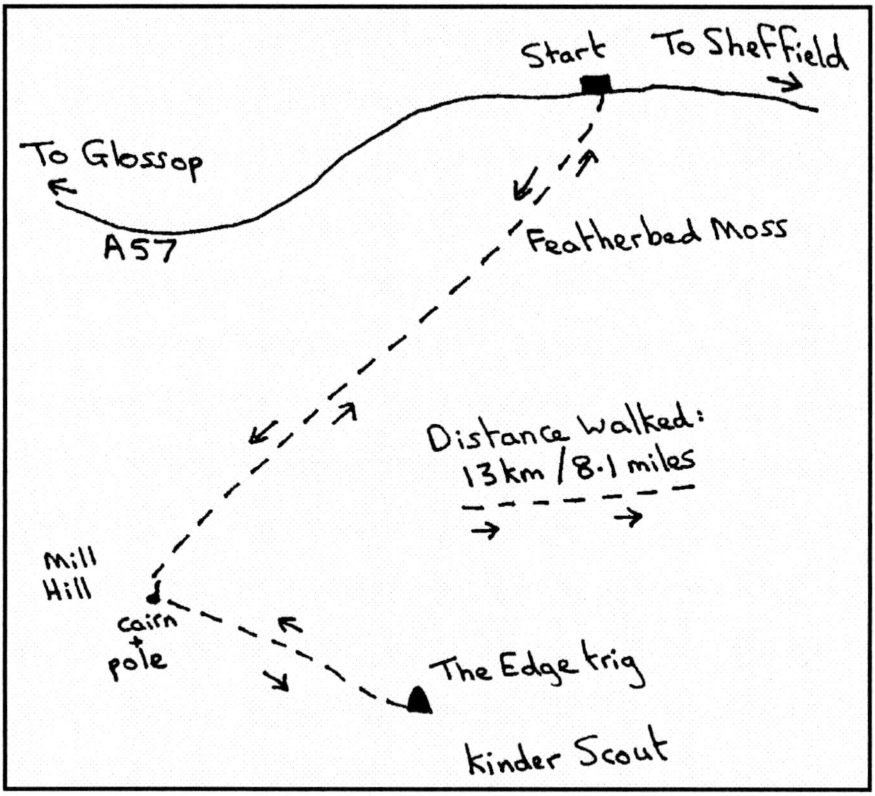

From the starting point on the A57, I headed south through the gate towards Kinder, following the sign for Ashop Moor. This well-laid path took me on a long, pleasant route over Featherbed Moss. I continued for just over two miles until reaching the path junction marked by a pole (SK 061904), where I turned left and headed towards Kinder.

Proceeding down the hill until I reached a cross-roads, here I went straight on and followed the route to Edale along the Pennine Way. There is a steep climb up to the Kinder plateau. Turning right at the top I followed the ridge-side path. After walking along the ridge for three quarters of a mile I was able to stand on a mound of rocks (SK 073891) and see the trig point, looking towards the north east.

To actually get to the trigpoint, I carried on the path until I came to a fence and instead of crossing over the stile, I turned left and followed the fence up the hill. When the fence came to an end, the trigpoint came into view (S3443). There are actually two trigs on this site, an old one that has toppled over and smashed and a shiny white replacement that sits atop a column of stones. Following the fence back down to the path and turning right, I took the same route back to the start point. Descending the path from Kinder, I took the path on the right when it forked in two and went straight on towards "Bleaklow" at the cross roads. I turned right when I reached the pole marker and the path took me back to the starting point.

Trigs to spot from the top:

Kinder Low: 2.3km to the south. **See page 30 of this book.**

Harry Hut: 3.5km to the north west. **See page 26 of this book.**

Brown Knoll: 4.3km to the south. **See page 14 of this book.**

Using the rocks in the Peak District

For hundreds of years, rocks have been extracted from the Peak District and put to use in many different ways. Quarries still exist within the national park, but the extraction of rock has been restricted since the area was designated a national park in 1951. And the use of the rocks has changed over time. Nowadays there is a big demand in garden centres for ornamental pieces of limestone and sandstone, while original mill wheels made from local gritstone are an expensive addition to several local gardens. A far cry from today's quirky visual uses, millstones were made from gritstone because of its' rough character and the fact that it was ideal for grinding up corn and producing flour. The flour that was generated in this process, however, was left looking grey and unappetising by the gritstone process and so was eventually abandoned. But this was not the end for the millstone made from local gritstone. With the emergence of the steel industry in Sheffield, millstones once again became incredibly useful for sharpening cutlery. Shale, on the other hand, was a vital ingredient in the production of cement. This means that both the predominant rocks in the Dark Peak have been useful to the local economy over the years and have actually helped to shape the industry found in this region.

Walk 4: Harry Hut

A mix of well used and less visible trails wind across Shaw Moor

Trig Point	Harry Hut at 440m/1444ft (SK 281431)	
Map	LR110,EOL1	
Distance	★☆☆☆☆	5.3km/3.3miles
Time	★★☆☆☆	1hr 25min
Ascent	★★☆☆☆	295m/967ft
Difficulty	★★★★☆	Some steep valley slopes
Start and Finish	Local road off the A624 with access to moor from it (SK 037921)	

ROUTE Plenty of local facilities are available at nearby Glossop to help stock up your picnic boxes before starting on this walk, or to rest and enjoy a drink when it's all over. This is the only one of our trigpoint walks that starts on the western side of Pennines.

Heading out of Glossop along the A624 after the junction with the A6016, the road bends to the right. Shortly after this, I took a local road on the left. The walk starts at the first bend where a path gives access to Shaw Moor.

Going over a style, the path initially heads along to the left but bends round and starts to climb the hill. I continued along this path until I came to a T-junction, with a larger path running from left to right. Here I took the path off to the right, climbing the ladder over the wall.

This new path heads over the top of Worm Stones and then continues along this route. At grid reference SK 043913 the walk comes to a junction of paths, with the trigpoint being on the route straight ahead. After a short climb up this path the trigpoint is reached (SK 045908).

After taking in the pleasant views over the moors, I then retraced my footsteps back down the path until reaching the intersection of paths. I needed to bear right here and pick up a path that is not well marked but it took me past the shooting cabin that comes into view here across the valley.

Harry Hut (SK 281431)

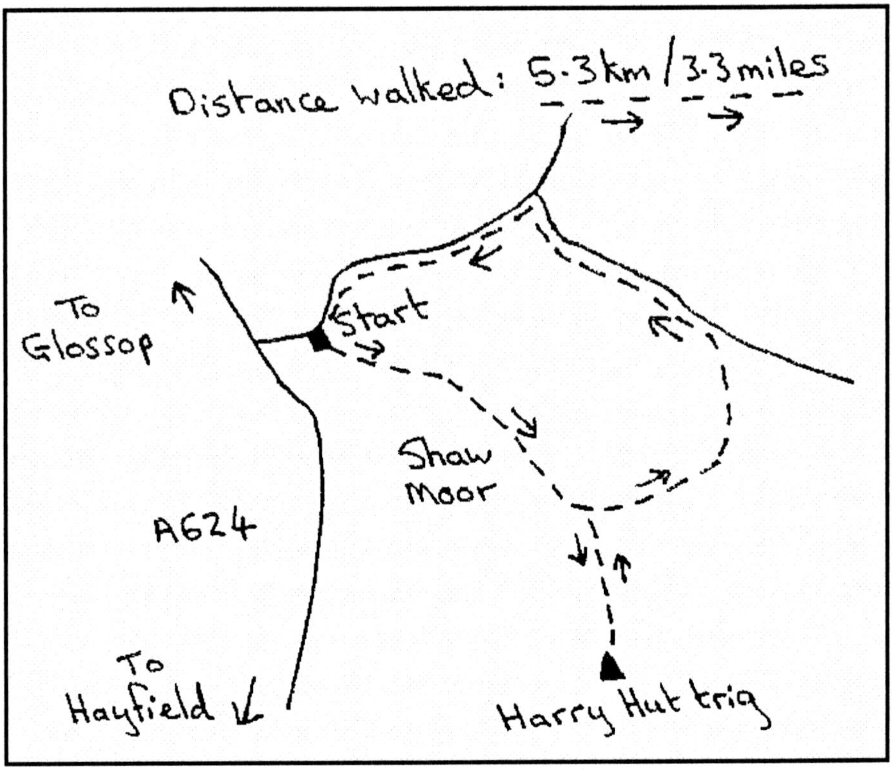

Heading into the valley before the cabin, the path is unmarked and steep but eventually leads to a crossing in the stream and to the other side of the river, where the going is generally better. This path now takes you past the left side of the cabin until it picks up a larger track, which the route follows. This track leads to a wall with a ladder, the route heading left here. Crossing over another ladder, the walk follows the track as it crosses the river, bears to the left and takes you over another ladder. Soon after the track comes out onto the road (SK 044925), where I turned left. This road took me back to the starting point.

Trigs to spot from the top:

Hollingworth Head: 1.4km to the west

Crown Edge Rocks: 2.6km to the north west. Now missing.

Lantern Pike: 3.5km to the south west

Peat in the Peaks

One of the key characteristics of the northern reaches of the Peak District are the peat bogs found on many Pennine moors. Good examples of rolling peat landscapes can be found on Kinder Scout, Ringinglow Bog and the area around Black Hill. Whilst undoubtedly a fascinating feature, peat landscapes can also be treacherous – especially after wet weather – so the utmost care is needed on them.

Tests have revealed most of the peat bogs in the area to have around three metres of peat lying on top of the bedrock. Some areas, however, have been found to have a staggering ten metres of peat covering the local rock underneath.

Heavy rain and the continual treading of walker's boots have caused problems for environmentally sensitive areas of peatlands in recent times. Erosion has been caused on most peat-based locations in the Peak District – a process that has been accentuated by heather burning in the region to preserve grouse stocks and acid rain caused by the growth of industry throughout Europe.

A great deal of experience is needed before walking around peat bogs. They can hide hidden traps several metres deep and are easy to get lost and disorientated in.

Walk 5: Kinder Low

A strenuous but hugely rewarding walk on Kinder.

Trig Point	Kinder Low at 633m (SK 079871)	
Map	LR110, EOL1	
Distance	★★★★☆	13.7km/8.3miles
Time	★★★★☆	4hrs
Ascent	★★★★☆	574m/1884ft
Difficulty	★★★★☆	Rocky terrain / steep in places
Start and Finish	Main car park at Edale (SK 124853)	

ROUTE This is a very strenuous walk, but one of the most rewarding in the Peak District, passing spectacular rock formations, streams and viewpoints. As with any walk on Kinder, I made sure that I took with me a compass, a map, sturdy shoes and waterproofs as the weather can turn for the worse at any time.

Parking is available in the main car park at Edale and from there I took the path to the left of the toilets which leads to the only road to the village. Turning right onto the road and continuing along it, I kept to the left of The Old Nag's Head pub. The road turns into a track, following signs for Grindsbrook and the route eventually takes a path to the right of a private drive. It then heads down the steps and crosses the bridge, joining a man-made path at the other side of the valley. The next step involved heading along this path and going through a gate that leads through a small wood and then out of the gate at the far side of it. I crossed the stream and continued along the path as it followed the right hand side of the river. A sheer cliff face eventually appears on the right, and this marks the spot when I had to carefully cross the river using the rocks and continue on the left hand side of it towards the top of the Kinder Plateau. Close to the top, the rocky river bed forks in two and then I headed to the left. I could now see a path straight in front of me as I emerged onto the top at grid reference SK105872. I took this stone path. As I followed this route along the edge of Kinder Scout I passed some incredible rock formations and enjoyed views to the south over the Peak District.

The path heads into a dip and crosses a stream, where I picked it up after the steep climb on the other side. Keeping to the main path and following the rocks, I went in a westerly direction. This path eventually brought me to a large cairn (SK 079865), where I took a path which almost doubled back on me up the hill to the right, and headed towards a collection of large rocks. Going past these rocks and entering a clearing I was able to see the trigpoint. After reaching it, I retraced my steps back

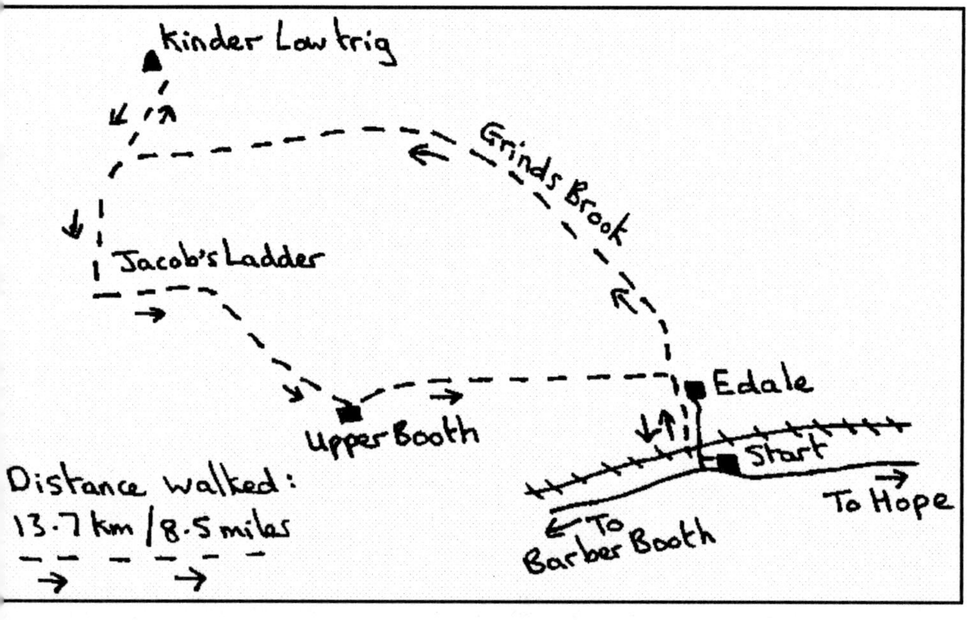

to the cairn, turning right onto the original path. Soon after, at SK 079864, I took a path off to the left, heading down the hill to a cross roads, where I turned left again. Heading down the path until reaching a cairn at SK 086862, I followed a path heading left down Jacobs Ladder. At the bottom, I crossed the footbridge over the river, heading through the gate and entering the National Trust land of Lee Farm, carrying along the path.Clearing a couple of styles and at SK 102852, I took a path off the road to the left towards Upper Booth Farm and Edale. Turning right out of the farm courtyard, I then immediately turned left and then right, following signs for Edale along the Pennine Way. I kept following the signs for Edale across the fields, heading over styles and through gates. When reaching Edale, I turned right onto the road and continued until just after the railway bridge, where a path to the left heads back into the car park.

Trigs to spot from the top:

Brown Knoll: 2km to the south. **See page 14 of this book.**

The Edge: 2.3km to the north. **See page 22 of this book.**

Harry Hut: 5.1km to the north west. **See page 26 of this book.**

Kinder Low (SK 079871)

The landslip at Mam Tor

One of the most dramatic landscapes in the country, let alone the Peak District, can be found at the foot of Mam Tor. The reason for this is the large landslip, which has left a 65 metre tall scar in the side of Mam Tor high above the A625 road, is the rock structure inside Mam Tor itself. At one time the A625 was the main link between Castleton and Manchester at the other side of the Pennines, but that all changed in 1979 when a large landslip crippled the road and made it impassable to traffic. Repairs to the road were deemed to be too expensive and so the road remains in the dramatic, cracked condition that Nature left it in. The debris that fell in the landslip can be easily spotted due to the differences of vegetation in the area. The more acidic gritstone and shale has darker vegetation growing on it than the limestone valley bottom, where light green grasses emerge. Today, vehicles heading from Castleton over the Pennines must wind their way up the steep Winnats Pass.

At the trigpoint atop Mam Tor, you will be standing over 600 metres above sea level and close to the earthworks of an iron age fort that was more than likely used to help locals escape and seek shelter during times of conflict. The make up of Mam Tor is the reason for the famous landslip – the alternating layers of sandstone and shale helped to create the instability, especially after heavy rain.

Walk 6: Mam Tor

An alternative walk to a popular trig point which has superb views of the Hope Valley

Trig Point	Mam Tor at 517m/1696ft (SK 127836)	
Map	LR110,EOL24	
Distance	✪✪✪✪✪	5.6km/3.5miles
Time	✪✪✪✪✪	1hr 30min
Ascent	✪✪✪✪✪	299m/981ft
Difficulty	✪✪✪✪✪	Initially steep but short climb
Start and Finish	Edale car park (SK 124853)	

ROUTE The starting point is the main car park at Edale. This can quickly fill up throughout the year, so it is advisable to get there in good time. I left the car park via the main entrance and turned left onto the road, where I got a good view of Mam Tor off to the right.

I continued along this road until I saw a public footpath on the right which is signed to Hollins Cross and took this new route. Carrying on along this path, I climbed over two stiles and headed past a farm building on the right. Before I got to the next farm building there was a footpath sign which sent me off to the right. I took this path up the hill, passing through a gate in the wall on the way. The path meets an intersection on the way to the top, where I followed the route left to the top of the hill. Here, as well as fine views, I found a memorial stone before turning right along the man-made path and heading to Mam Tor.

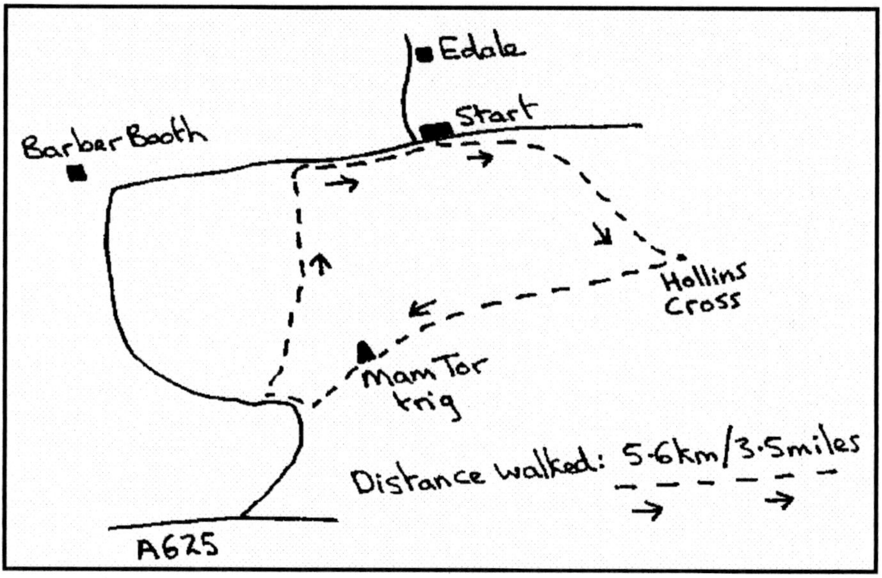

After walking through a gate, the path took me up to the trigpoint (S4230), where I was able to enjoy fine views of Hope Valley. Continuing on the path past the trigpoint, I dropped down to the road and once at the road I turned right along it up the slope. The road bends round to the right and soon I saw a bus stop on the right with a gate that I went through. Immediately after the gate a path on the left heads directly down the hill and this is the one I followed, heading through two gates and continuing along this path. Soon after I saw a gate on the left marked "private" and shortly after this will be another gate on the same side that I went through, following the sign to Edale which took me right down a concrete track. At the bottom of the track the route turned right on the road and continued until I reached the car park, which I found on the left.

Trigs to spot from the top:

Bradwell Moor: 3.5km to the south.

Edale Moor: 4.2km to the north. **See page 18 of this book.**

Brown Knoll: 4.7km to the west. **See page 14 of this book.**

Walk 7: Winhill Pike

Win Hill is an unmistakable landmark that provides incredible views.

Trig Point	Winhill Pike at 462m/1516ft (SK 186850)	
Map	LR110, EOL1	
Distance	✪✪✪○○	8.5km/5.3miles
Time	✪✪○○○	2hr 5mins
Ascent	✪✪✪○○	476m/1561ft
Difficulty	✪✪✪○○	Very Steep, often muddy climb
Start and Finish	Yorkshire Bridge, off A6013 (SK 198849)	

ROUTE Win Hill's triangular summit is an unmistakable landmark seen for many miles around and provides incredible views. The walk I embarked on to reach this trigpoint started at the Yorkshire Bridge—the actual bridge to be found off the A6013 and not the pub of the same name on the main road. Crossing the bridge, which goes over the River Derwent, I then turned right onto the track. Soon after going through a gate, I took a path off to the left which is sign-posted for "Win Hill." Following the steep and often muddy path up through Parkin Clough, I crossed over a couple of forestry tracks as I climbed to the top of Win Hill. This was a steep, direct climb but one which brings quick rewards to everyone in the form of excellent views of the Peak District, and in particular Ladybower Reservoir.

Trigs to spot from the top:

High Neb: 4.1km to the east. **See page 40 of this book.**

Abney Moor: 5.7km to the south.

Back Tor: 6km to the north. **See page 56 of this book.**

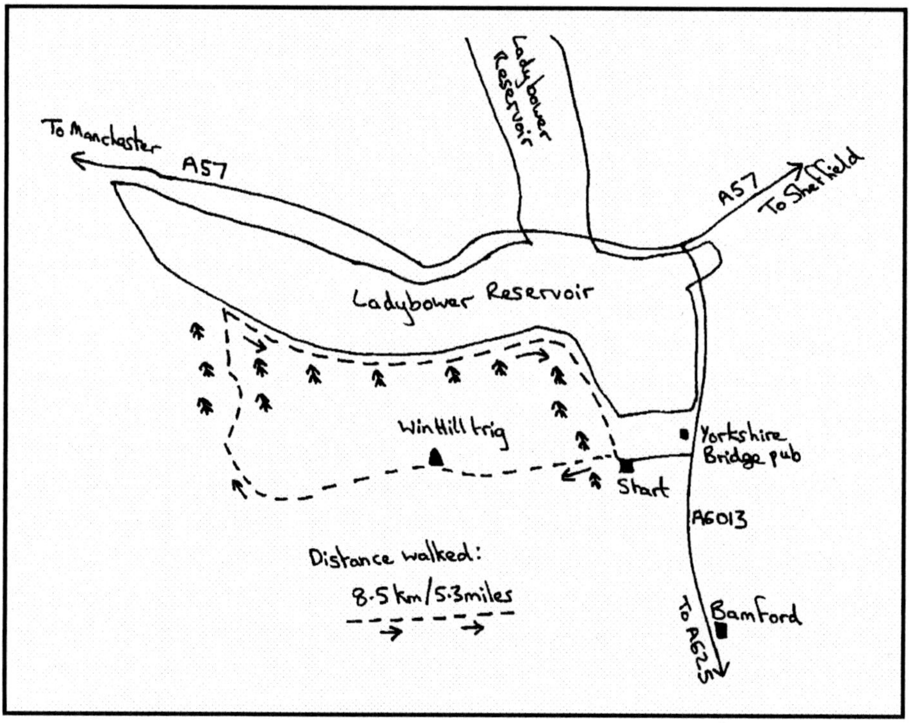

When I reached a fence, I climbed the stile and again followed signs for "Win Hill," with just one more stile to climb before I reached the trigpoint (S4228) at the walk's highest point. Unfortunately, before my visit the trig had been vandalised but the views out to Ladybower, Mam Tor and the Hope Valley were worth the climb.

A path continues on the left side of the trig, which I followed. I then branched off to the right at the fork in the path soon after Win Hill and kept to this main path as it bent to the right on the top of the moor.

Eventually the path started to run along the right side of a wall, with a stile to climb when the wall left the route. The route follows the path straight on until you reach a ruined wall. I turned right at this point towards the Woodlands Valley coniferous plantation.

My walk took me through the gate and I followed the footpath sign straight on into the wood, heading down on a forestry track. Through another gate, I followed the footpath signs straight down the hillside until I was brought out at Ladybower Reservoir. Once clear of the woods, I turned right onto the main track and followed the reservoir-side route until it took me back to the Yorkshire Bridge.

Winhill Pike (SK 186850)

Peak District fact: The National Park is home to 8,756km of dry stone wall.

Peak District fact: There are 105 Conservation Areas situated inside the National Park boundary.

The role of water in the national park

The Peak District National Park is the second most visited national park in the whole world, coming in a few million visitors short of Japan's Mount Fuji. There is good reason why these two parks are the most popular amongst tourists – they are easy to get to and they have millions of people living close by. In Mount Fuji's case it's the metropolis of Tokyo that keeps visitor numbers high, and in the Peak District that job is done by the people of Sheffield, Manchester, Leeds and Nottingham. The park is hemmed in by major cities, with millions of people living within an easy drive. These people use the Peak District for recreational reasons – and they have also come to depend on the hills for their source of clean water.

Thanks to its' upland location, the Peak District has a higher than average rainfall and a series of sparsely populated valleys that were able to house several large reservoirs. Standing at the top of Win Hill, the trigpoint affords a tremendous view of Ladybower Reservoir, which stretches both to the west and also under the road bridge to the north. Further up the Derwent Valley from this point can be found Derwent Reservoir and Howden Reservoir, both distinguishable by their twin tower, ornate dam walls that were used as practice runs by the Dambuster Squadron during the Second World War in preparation for their famous raids on the German water infrastructure.

Walk 8: High Neb

A popular 'there and back' walk along well worn paths on Stanage Edge

Trig Point	High Neb at 458m/1502ft (SK 228853)	
Map	LR110,EOL1	
Distance	✪✪✩✩✩	6.1km/3.8miles
Time	✪✪✩✩✩	1hr 35min
Ascent	✪✩✩✩✩	151m/494ft
Difficulty	✪✪✩✩✩	Worn paths with moderate climbs
Start and Finish	Off road parking on the A57 (SK 230879)	

ROUTE This can be a very busy route, so I was sure to set out early so I could get one of the few off-road parking spaces on the A57 at Moscar (SK 230879).

From here, I took the short path towards the moorside fence, turning right at the first stile onto the track leading to Hallam Moors. This track took me up to the ridge known as Stanage Edge. It first heads through a gap in an old wall, which I went through instead of taking the path off to the right. Once through the wall, I had a choice of heading left or right, and I followed the top of the ridge off to the right. This walk along the ridge takes a route onto the top of the Stanage Edge rocks, where there is a good chance of seeing climbers scaling their tough challenge. It was a straight forward walk now up to the trigpoint at High Neb.In good condition, the trigpoint (S2157) offers great views to the west, taking in Win Hill and the hills around Hope Valley. From the trigpoint the walk retraced its' steps back along Stanage Edge. I followed the path until it entered a dip in the land (SK 226866), where I went left through the old wall past a stone marker with the letters "WW" on it. Shortly after, I turned right onto the original path and followed this back to the starting point.

Trigs to spot from the top:

Stanage Edge: 3.3km to the south east. **See page 52 of this book.**

Winhill Pike: 4.1km to the west. **See page 36 of this book.**

Rod Moor: 4.6km to the north east.

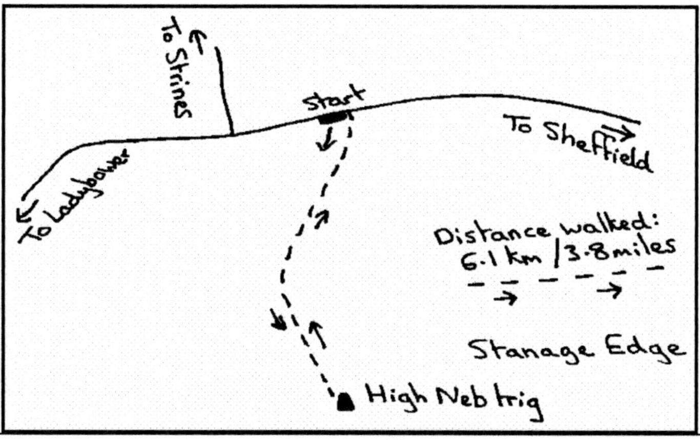

Walk 9: Kirk Edge

A walk across the National Park's boundary to a low-key and hidden trigpoint on Onesmoor.

Trig Point	Kirk Edge at 393m/1296ft (SK 277929)	
Map	LR110, EOL1	
Distance	★★☆☆☆	4.5km/2.8miles
Time	★☆☆☆☆	50mins
Ascent	★☆☆☆☆	77m/253ft
Difficulty	★☆☆☆☆	Straightforward short walk
Start and Finish	Local road nr Carmelite Convent (SK 285921)	

ROUTE On the eastern edge of the Peak District, this walk travels across the national park's boundary with the aim of finding the Kirk Edge trig. Parking on the local road just west of Carmelite Convent, I took the path from the road heading north onto a grassy field. Initially, the path followed a wall with a small deciduous woodland on the other side of it.

Once I reached the end of the wall, the public right of way continued straight ahead, although it was at times difficult to make out underfoot. I continued walking straight ahead until I reached the wall and then turned right and followed the wall until I found a stile embedded in it.

Trigs to spot from the top:

Emlin Ridge: 3.8km to the west.

Loxley Common: 4km to the south east. **To be featured in Trigpoint Walks in the Peak District: The National Park Fringe**

Rod Moor: 4.6km north east.

I climbed the stile and then headed across the often boggy field to the steps that brought me out onto the road, known as Onesmoor Bottom. On a clear day, this stretch of the walk will treat walkers to some far-reaching views of Sheffield and several power stations as the flat, eastern land stretches out towards the Humber Estuary.

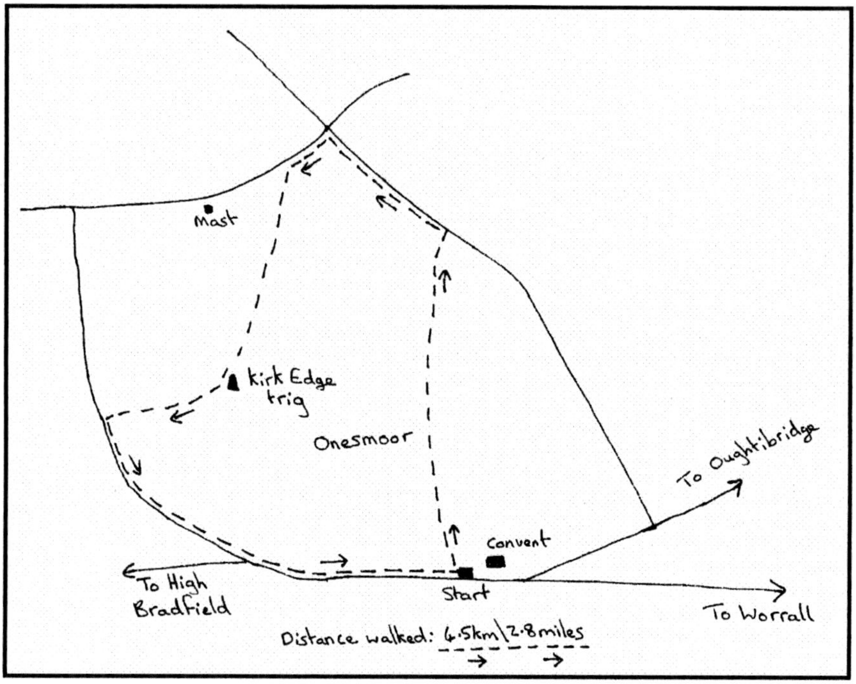

Once at the road, the route turns left and heads in a north-westerly direction until reaching a cross-roads where it takes in an historic milestone, as well as views out to Stocksbridge and the Emley Moor broadcasting mast. I took the left-hand turn onto Onesacre Road, where I soon came across a path on the left, initially leading through a small woodland.

Following the path, I hopped over a stile into another field and then cleared two newly created styles across a track until I approached a dry stone wall on the top of the hill. Climbing over the steps on this wall, I was able to see the discreetly placed trigpoint on the left. The trigpoint is now surrounded by futuristic-looking buildings, aerials and radars that assist Sheffield University's Astronomy Department to carry out research. This must be one of the more unusual trigpoint locations.

I continued down the hill in a westerly direction towards the gate, which lead me onto the road. I turned left at this road and then left at the first junction. This takes the walk back to the start point. As this is a short walk, I found myself with time to take a trip to nearby High Bradfield. This is always a rewarding diversion to the centre of one of the country's largest parishes and a quaint, picturesque Peak District village.

Kirk Edge, Onesmoor (SK 277929)

Peak District fact: Close to Manchester and Sheffield, it is a highly accessible National Park

Peak District fact: The National Park covers a massive area of 1,438km², which is 555 square miles.

My Trigpoint Notes…

Walk 10: Ox Stones

A steady round walk along Burbage Moor and Burbage Rocks.

Trig Point	Ox Stones at 419m/1375ft (SK 281431)
Map	LR110,EOL1
Distance	✪✪☆☆☆ 7.2km/4.5miles
Time	✪☆☆☆☆ 1hr 35min
Ascent	✪✪☆☆☆ 282m/925ft
Difficulty	✪✪☆☆☆ Easy paths but rocky in places
Start and Finish	Car park next to footpath at Lady Canning's Plantation (SK 278834)

ROUTE This is an area, like many in the Peak District, that can be extremely different through the seasons. Taking this walk in the summer may see walkers treated to T-shirt weather and the prospect of collecting an ice cream from the van often found near Burbage Brook. In winter, however, walkers may have to deal with snow blizzards and icy roads.

From the car park, I crossed the road and entered the path into Burbage Moor at the side of Lady Canning's Plantation. Instead of taking the main path straight ahead, I immediately branched off on the path to the right. This led up to Ox Stones, an interesting rock formation worthy of a visit in itself.

Once the stones are reached, the trigpoint (S2159) is visible and easily accessible.

From the concrete trig, I made my way across the open moorland back down to the main path in front of the trees. Once there, I turned right onto the path and continued until I went past the plantation and into a slight dip, where I turned right at the intersection of the paths. This is a well-used and historic track, known as Houndkirk Road. The milestone passed on the right is a reminder of times in which it was a more important route.

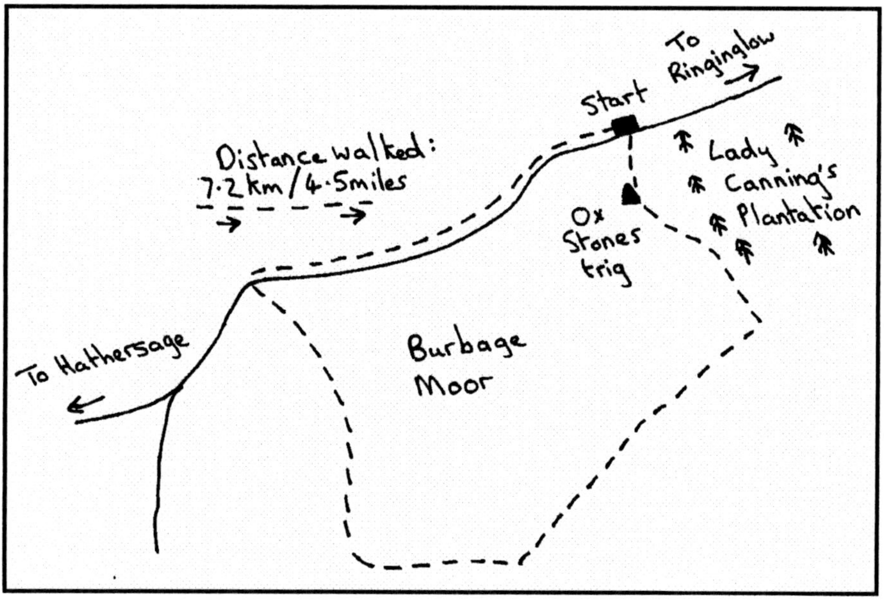

I continued along the track until I reached another intersection, following the clearly marked footpath sign to the right. When I reached a way-marker indicating another crossroads, I took the path to the right.

Continuing along this path, I walked straight on over the stream that flows into Burbage Brook and climbed up onto the tops of Burbage Rocks. From here I could see over to Stanage Edge, the site of another trigpoint walk featured in this book. This established path skirts along the western edge of Burbage Moor and brought me out at Upper Burbage Bridge, where I turned right and followed the road back to the starting point. I used the path on the left hand side of the road as it heads up over the moor.

Trigs to spot from the top:

Ringinglow: 2km to the east.

Blacka Plantation: 2.3km to the south east

Stanage Edge: 2.9km to the west. **See page 52 of this book.**

Peak District fact: The Peak District National Park is the second most visited park in the world, behind Japan's Mount Fuji National Park.

Peak District fact: There are 38,000 people living within the park boundary.

WALK 11: Stanedge Pole

A short and accessible walk to a missing trigpoint

Trig Point	Stanedge Pole at 438m/1437ft (SK 246844)	
Map	LR110,EOL1	
Distance	★☆☆☆☆	2.9km/1.8miles
Time	★☆☆☆☆	45mins
Ascent	★☆☆☆☆	92m/299ft
Difficulty	★★☆☆☆	Accessible and well used route
Start and Finish	Redmires Reservoirs, Redmires Road (SK256853)	

ROUTE Although there is physically no actual trigpoint up at Stanedge Pole there is one marked on the Ordnance Survey 1:25,000 map. And this is a pleasant enough walk to justify a visit to the large pole, which can be seen from miles around and therefore also commands some fantastic views.

Parking at the very end of Redmires Road, I then took the track which turns off to the right of the road and leads all the way up to Stanedge Pole. A byway, this route is open to all traffic and can cause problems for walkers. Motorbike scramblers and 4x4 recreational users are a common sight on this section of the walk and even when walkers don't have to dodge them you can see their impact in the widespread and annoying erosion they have caused. On wet days eroded gulleys will fill with water and access may be very sludgy. Following this track all the way until I reached the unmistakable pole, I passed through a gate on the way as the wood on the right gave way to moorland. The pole itself is surrounded by rocks which have been carved into by many lovers over the decades.

On a clear day from here, the views extend to some of the most glorious and memorable sights in the Peak District, including Mam Tor, Win Hill and Kinder Scout. From Stanedge Pole you can also see the other two trigpoints on Stanage Edge, with High Neb on the right and Stanage Edge on the left.

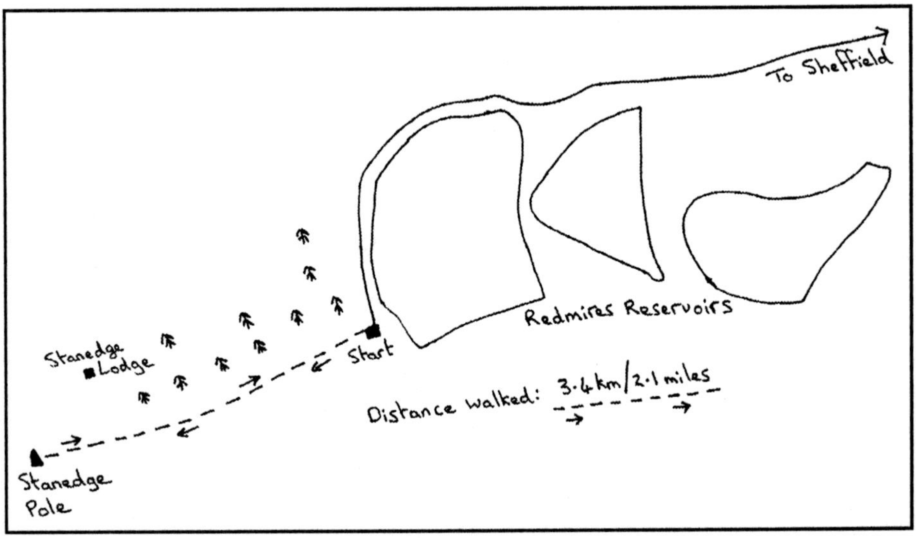

On the way back down the hill I enjoyed the views towards Sheffield over Redmires Reservoirs. For hungry walkers who have brought a packed lunch, there is a picnic site in a small wooded area on the left side, close to the first corner as the road heads back towards the city.

I have described three separate walks to add a variety of approaches onto the edge. These various routes allow walkers to become familiar with this area. I retraced my footsteps down the path I went up to reach the starting point.

Peak District fact: There are a staggering 2,893 listed buildings that are protected inside the National Park.

WALK 12 : Stanage Edge

Fantastic views abound on this short but rewarding walk

Trig Point	Stanage Edge at 457m/1499ft (SK 250830)	
Map	LR110, EOL1	
Distance	✪✪✩✩✩	3.4km/2.1miles
Time	✪✩✩✩✩	45mins
Ascent	✪✩✩✩✩	113m/370ft
Difficulty	✪✪✩✩✩	A few moderate climbs
Start and Finish	Car park on road west of Ringinglow (SK 260830)	

ROUTE There are many stunning views to be found on this walk, starting with the one I was treated to at the car park. The scenery of Burbage Brook and Burbage Rocks are mouthwatering on warm summer days and strangely addictive even in poor weather, when mist, rain and snow can add a very different charm.

From the car park at grid reference SK 260830, I headed for the road and turned left onto it. As the road bent away to the left, I followed a path heading off on the right, going past the sign declaring it to be open country. Continuing along the route as it wound a way onto the top of the rocks, I was happy to see it turn into a nice and easy man-made path. The trigpoint (S2156) is seen soon after and affords great views towards Hope Valley and along Stanage Edge. Standing on a delicately balanced rock, it really gave me a fine vantage point.

I continued along the path past the trigpoint until I saw a path off to the left at grid reference SK 250830. Taking this path, it took me down to the bottom of Stanage Edge. At a fork in the path, I took the track off to the right which led me down to the road and I turned left onto it. The road soon bent round to the left and after this I saw a stile on the right which I climbed over. Immediately after climbing the fence I saw a choice of three paths in the grass and I took the one on the left, following it until it brought me out at another road. At that point, I climbed over the stile onto the road and just to the right across the road I saw another stile leading to the next path.

Trigs to spot from the top:

Ox Stones: 2.9km to the east. **See page 46 of this book.**

High Neb: 3.3km to the north west. **See page 40 of this book.**

Blacka Plantation: 4.3km to the south east.

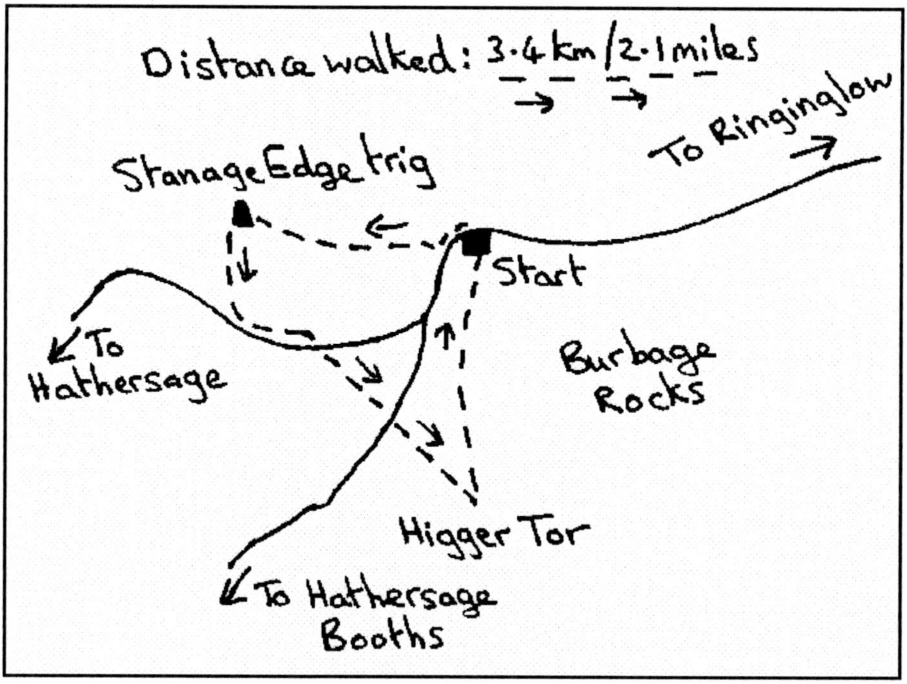

This took me up towards Higger Tor and I stuck to this route until I saw a path on the left at grid reference SK 257821, where I needed to branch off. With nice views of Burbage Brook on the right, this path took me over a series of rocks before dropping down into the car park where I started.

Peak District fact: The main industries in the park are tourism, farming and quarrying.

Peak District fact: The National Park has over 74,000ha of Environmentally Sensitive Areas.

Tors

These distinctive features of the Peak District landscape are popular among both walkers and photographers. The walk to Back Tor rewards us with a peak of spectacular rock and also the chance to catch other views to the north and south in this amazing part of the country. But what actually is a tor? The basic definition of a tor is an isolated mass of bare rock. This can be of various sizes, there is no definite rule in respect of that. But a tor can be clearly identified with the eye, the landform being a prominent exposure of rock found at the top of peaks throughout Derbyshire.

As for how tors form, there is a lot of debate among the experts. There are several factors that could be responsible for carving these rock sculptures into the landscape, or indeed it could be a combination of different factors. One possibility is that tors are created by the forces of weathering, with wind and rain battering the ground to expose the rock and, once it has, forging it into the strange shapes and patterns that we see today. Large blocks of gritstone could also have been exposed by massive landslips in times gone by. The constant freezing and thawing of rainwater throughout the winter also has the ability to open up and develop cracks in the rock, separating what would later become the tor from the bedrock.

WALK 13 : Back Tor

A short, sharp climb up to one of the most dramatic trigpoints in the Peak District

Trig Point	Back Tor at 538m/1765ft (SK 198910)	
Map	LR110, OL1	
Distance	✪✪○○○	5.6km/3.7miles
Time	✪○○○○	1hr 20mins
Ascent	✪✪○○○	268m/880ft
Difficulty	✪✪✪○○	Rocky terrain in places
Start and Finish	Car park at Strines Bridge (SK 220909)	

ROUTE A short, sharp climb up to one of the most dramatic trigpoints in the Peak District, the trip up to Back Tor is well worth making. Although round walks can be organised from the western approaches, I attempted this "there and back" walk as it allowed a visit to the Strines area and saved a nice venture along Derwent Valley for walks elsewhere in this book.

There is a sizable car park at Strines Bridge but sadly there have been more and more thefts from vehicles parked in there during recent years. This is a trend that is increasing across the area, unfortunately, so you need to be aware and cover up any valuables you have to leave in your car. The route from the car park wound up a concrete path from the far side of it, passing through the middle of a tree plantation. After following this for 800m, I passed through the gate and then took the track which led to the right rather than continuing on the concrete track. This route leads to the top of the moor, within sight of the impressive tor. Sticking closely to the path, I took great care as I walked up because the higher I got, the rockier the route became.

After rain this can also be a hazardous journey. The track to the top starts high above Foulstone Dike as it flows into Strines Reservoir, but then actually starts to shadow the route of smaller streams and can be become very muddy and slippy.

Back Tor (SK 198910)

The route to the top eventually levelled out at Bradfield Head Gate (SK 198907), a stone post that signifies the parish boundary. At this point, I was relieved to find a stone path crossing the way from left to right. I took the newly-laid path to the right at this intersection, heading in a northerly direction until reaching Back Tor. The trigpoint (S2145) is one well-worth reaching, but care is needed to scramble onto rocks in order to get to it. On a fine day the views from here are really astounding, looking westward to Win Hill, Lose Hill and Mam Tor, and enjoying the sight of Sheffield to east. On a poor day, however, walkers will be lucky to see their own feet in the mist and, even if they can, the wind may blow them clean over. Careful use of a map and compass may be needed. Once I reached the trig, I retraced my steps back to the car park, of course remembering to turn left back down the main path at Bradfield Head Gate.

Trigs to spot from the top:

Margery Hill: 4.8km north. **See page 64 of this book.**

Emlin Ridge: 4.8km to the north east.

Winhill Pike: 6km to the south. **See page 36 of this book.**

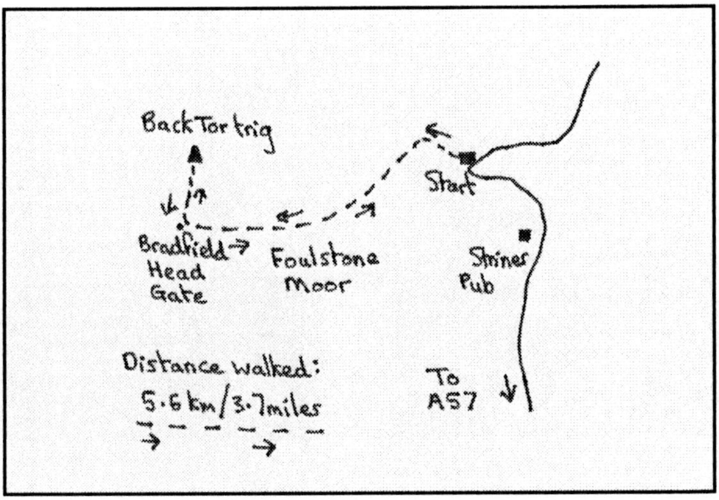

Derwent Valley dams

One of the biggest tourist pulls of the Dark Peak and the centre of several trigpoint walks in this book is The Derwent Valley. With a popular road turning north off the A57, the route is dominated by a series of reservoirs that are vital for the area's water and recreation. They changed the face of the valley in the first half of the twentieth century. Ladybower, Derwent and Howden Reservoirs were constructed by the Derwent Valley Water Board to fill the taps of people in Sheffield, Derby and Nottingham. Howden and Derwent were built between 1901 and 1916, both sporting dam walls of locally quarried millstone grit that was transported into the valley on a special railway line that has now been dismantled. While construction was ongoing, as many as 500 people were housed in a specially built working village, known locally as Tin Town, and remains of this historic settlement are visible as the road edges past Derwent Reservoir. Ladybower was added later, between 1935 and 1945, and now straddles the A57.

Although popular in the modern day, the reservoirs were controversial at the time they were built. The hamlets Derwent and Ashopton had to be abandoned, along with 22 farmsteads in what was a near total clearance of the valley. Families were rehoused in dwellings close to the Yorkshire Bridge pub, while those buried in the local graveyard were exhumed and laid to rest once more in Bamford.

Walk 14: Higher Shelf Stones

A walk across open country through a disorientating peat landscape – Bleaklow is to be approached with caution.

Trig Point	Higher Shelf Stones at 621m/2037ft (SK 088947)	
Map	LR119, EOL24	
Distance	★★☆☆☆	7.6km/4.7miles
Time	★★☆☆☆	1hr 45mins
Ascent	★★☆☆☆	248m/815ft
Difficulty	★★★★☆	Difficult route over open country
Start and Finish	Car park at Doctor's Gate on the A57 (SK 096928)	

ROUTE Bleaklow has been so named for a good reason. In bad weather it can get very bleak!

Higher Shelf Stones (SK 088947)

As much of this walk relies on following compass directions and making a steady way across open country without the help of obvious paths, I heeded the advice of other walkers and did not set out on this trigpoint hunt if the weather was looking bad or as if it could turn for the worse. Mist can descend on the area around Bleaklow extremely quickly and can turn a leisurely stroll into a nightmare. This walk does not go to Bleaklow itself, but the whole area needs to be treated with respect.

The walk starts at Doctor's Gate (SK 096928) and I headed through the gate signalling the start of National Trust land, following the path with a stream on the left. I continued on the path as it crossed the stream and followed it until I reached a crossroads marked by a pole, turning right here to join the Pennine Way. This is a well used path and is on laid stone in parts. I followed it until one of the stone sections ended and after a small dip I found a stone marker pointing the way straight ahead. A second stone marker soon offered a choice of paths left and right and I went left here.

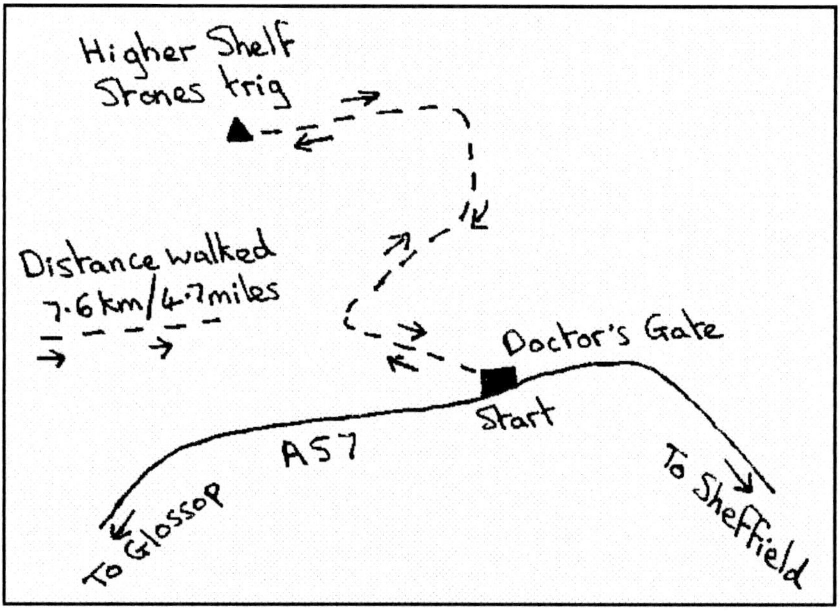

I followed the path to a clearing where another marker sent me off to the left to join another man-made path. When the path came to an end a marker directed me to the right and I picked up another path 20 metres on. This one bent round to the left into Hern Clough and crossed the stream at the top of the valley.

I followed the path until I reached a stone Pennine Way marker (SK 096948) which identified the point at which I left the path and climbed the bank on the left. From this point I could see Higher Shelf Stones lying in a westerly direction. This is an area of open country and I needed to make my way west from here, heading for the top of the hill where I found the trigpoint.

There is no obvious path leading to the top, although I did find tracks (such as the one at SK 094948) that make the route easier. I took care over the often uneven peat landscape, which can be dangerous. As I climbed onto the top of the hill I could start to see aircraft debris, a grim reminder of an accident involving an RAF plane which took place on this hill during World War Two. I headed beyond the wreckage as the trigpoint (S2627) is located to the south west of the crash site at grid reference SK 088947. From it I could enjoy views over Glossop and over to Kinder Scout as it was a clear day.

Trigs to spot from the top:

Cock Hill: 3.3km north west.

West End Moor: 4.3km to the south east. **See page 71 of this book.**

Hey Edge: 5.4km north.

The return route follows the same path, so I headed back over to Hern Clough by going over the moor in an easterly direction. If you pick up one of several tracks, make sure it is heading east. At the stone marker, I turned right onto the path and followed the stone markers back on the original path. When I reached the crossroads marked by a pole (SK 089933) I turned left and headed back down to the starting point at Doctor's Gate.

Peak District fact: The moorland in the National Park adds up to nearly 51,000ha.

A dam perfect park

Elsewhere in the book we have talked about the construction of reservoirs in the Peak District, but let's turn our attention to why the Dark Peak is such an ideal location for them. Firstly, the clue to the success of the reservoirs lies in the local rock. The shale valleys are ideal for trapping water because they are impermeable. The steep slopes of the valley are also useful because they make it easy to build a dam wall and help the reservoir to fill up. The Pennines are also the first set of hills to receive the prevailing westerly wet winds that enter the country from over the Atlantic. If you add all these things up, you get a dam perfect place to house reservoirs and provide a good water supply to the millions of people living nearby the Peak District.

Walk 15: Margery Hill

A long walk with some steep climbs, this route takes in some glorious scenery around the reservoirs of Derwent Valley.

Trig Point	Margery Hill at 546m/1791ft (SK 189957)	
Map	LR110, EOL1	
Distance	✪✪✪✪✪	18.2km/11.3miles
Time	✪✪✪✪○	4hrs 40mins
Ascent	✪✪✪○○	555m/1821ft
Difficulty	✪✪✪✪○	Long walk with steep climbs
Start and Finish	Car park at Fairholmes in the Derwent Valley (SK 172891)	

ROUTE For this one, I parked in the public car park at Fairholmes and headed towards the facilities block, where I could pick up a path for Derwent Dam. The path led onto a concrete road, from which I followed a route round to the right as the impressive dam wall came into view on the left.

Turning off the road through a gate on the left which led me towards the dam, I headed up the steps on the right when I got there. At the top I needed to turn left onto a short path and then left again through a kissing gate, starting a lengthy walk alongside Derwent Reservoir, which was on the left. I continued on this water-side walk as it eventually ventured across a bridge and through a gate.

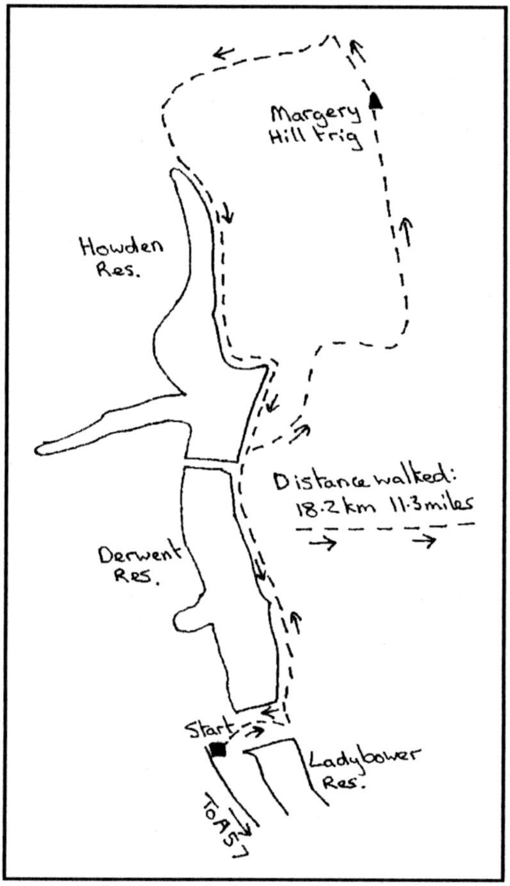

Just after the gate, I took a path on the right that cut back on itself (SK 171921) and rose up through the trees. The route went through a gate into the National Trust's Nether Hey. Going through a second gate at the brow of the hill, the walk went past a stone marker commemorating a CPRE Merit Award and followed the path off to the right. This path led up to Featherbed Moss and I climbed a stile near the top where the land was more peat-based. Ignoring paths off to the right that climbed to the top of Featherbed Moss, I instead stuck to the ridgeside main path which headed north towards Margery Hill. I soon came across a cairn on the path, from which the trigpoint could be seen. When I got close to the trigpoint, I left the path on the right to get to the top of Margery Hill. It was a clear day and I was able to see a wind farm in the north as well as the two transmission masts, Holme Moss and Emley Moor.

Trigs to spot from the top:

Outer Edge: 1.8km north west. **See page 68 of this book.**

Back Tor: 4.8km south. **See page 56 of this book.**

Emlin Ridge: 5.6km to the south east.

From the trigpoint, I returned to the path, turning right onto it and continuing in the direction I was originally heading in. I walked past Margery Hill Cairn, fenced off by the National Trust, until the path came to a cross roads marked by a large cairn.

Turning left here, I followed a well-established path back down into Derwent Valley. I wound down with the path down as it hugged the route of small streams, eventually turning off to the right and continuing to where two rivers meet (SK 175952). At this point, I crossed the river and continued ahead.

Still following the rivers downhill, I needed to cross over a bridge and then I followed the path straight on as the sign pointed to the Derwent

Margery Hill (SK 189957)

Valley. This path now took me on the left side of both Howden Reservoir and Derwent Reservoir and is a very popular route.

Just before I got to the second set of dam wall towers at the end of Derwent Reservoir, I saw a path off to the right through a kissing gate, which I took. Turning right down to the bottom of the steps (there are 110), I made my way left across the field towards the road. I turned right onto the road, heading over the bridge and taking the path off to the left back to the car park.

The Edges

A haven for local climbers in the Peak District are the popular "edges" that occur high up at the top of several valleys. Perhaps the best example is Stanage Edge, which forms the base of three walks featured in this book. On the top of the edge there are good, well-used paths to trigpoints with great views and the chances are you'll also meet the odd climber or two as you go. Left by rivers that wore away the landscape, the edges now stand out as a testimony to weathering that took thousands of years. The wearing away of weak sandstone at the base of the edges causes gritstone to occasionally collapse – leading to the collection of fallen rocks at the foot of the edge. Some of these were successfully used to create millstones, with less successful attempts being abandoned and still visible today.

Walk 16 : Outer Edge

Remote and exposed Howden Moor is the setting for this difficult and demanding walk

Trig Point	Outer Edge at 541m/1775ft (SK 177969)	
Map	LR110,EOL1	
Distance	✪✪○○○	15km/9.3miles
Time	✪✪✪○○	3hrs 30min
Ascent	✪✪✪✪✪	854m/2803ft
Difficulty	✪✪✪○○	Top of moors often boggy
Start and Finish	Car park at Midhope at entrance to Langsett Wood and Reservoir (SK 213995)	

ROUTE From the car park, I followed the track down towards Langsett Wood and went through the gate. This lengthy track took me through another gate and bent to the right before another gate took me out into open country. Just after this gate I walked between two old, ruined buildings, sticking to the main path straight ahead. On the right I could see the Emley Moor mast and a windfarm.

The path eventually came to a T junction at grid reference SK 197001, where I took the path to the left. This path carries on up the hill before heading down into a valley and then going off to the left along the ridge of Mickledon Edge. Soon after I came across a signpost, where I continued straight ahead and followed the route for Derwent and Ashop Valley.

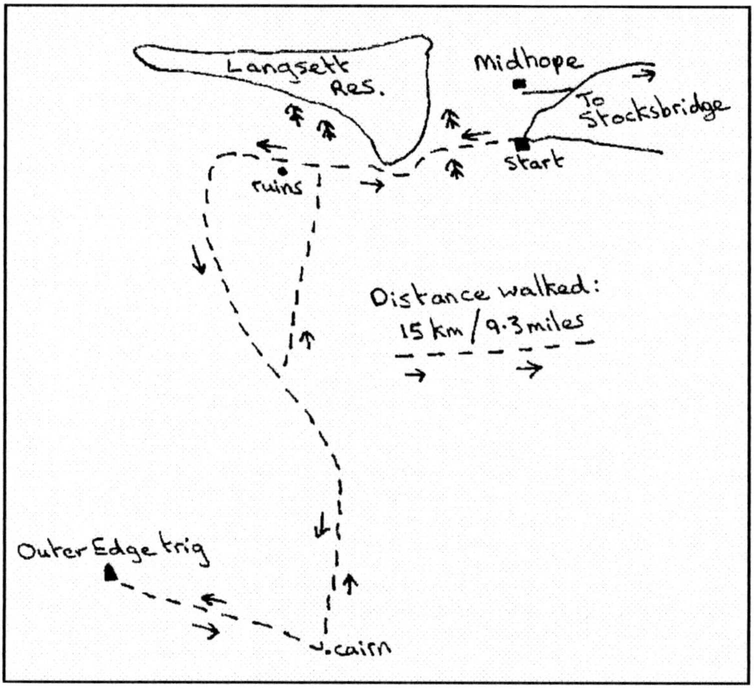

As I climbed to around 1460ft, I could notice the change of ground conditions as I entered the peat zone with numerous examples of gritstone. The path went past a cairn at SK 192971 and it is here that the amazing views started to appear. A second cairn has been built at SK 185960, and here the route met another path and turned right along it. This section of the route can be very boggy and care is needed, but it led me up to the trigpoint at SK 177969. The trig is unusual in that it has a memorial plaque on it for a dog called Penny.

From the trigpoint, I returned back the way I came, turning left onto the original path at the cairn. Then I headed along the path down the hill until I saw a path off to the right with a signpost to Langsett at SK 191987. I took this as it provided an alternative walk back. This path brought me out at a gate, where I turned right and retraced my steps along the original track back to the car park.

Trigs to spot from the top:

Margery Hill: 1.8km to the south east. **See page 64 of this book.**

South Nab: 3.9km to the north west. **See page 77 of this book.**

West End Moor: 6.1km to the south west. **See page 71 of this book.**

Caves

The real home of caves in the Peak District is the White Peak. The limestone found in the area has been carved by underground streams and rivers to house a complex system of fascinating caves. But despite housing the majority, there are good examples in the Dark Peak. Don't attempt to explore on your own, but guided tours are available in Castleton's Treak Cliff Cavern and the Blue John Cavern.

Walk 17: West End Moor

A long but rewarding walk through woodland and moorland to give fine views over Alport Castles.

Trig Point	West End Moor at 504m/1772ft (SK 129932)
Map	LR110, EOL1
Distance	✪✪✪✪✪ 16.3km/10.1miles
Time	✪✪✪✪○ 4hrs 35min
Ascent	✪✪✪○○ 568m/1865ft
Difficulty	✪✪✪○○ Some steep climbs
Start and Finish	Car park at Fairholmes, Derwent Valley (SK 204865)

ROUTE This is a lengthy, enjoyable walk which cuts through woodland and moorland to give some impressive Peak District views.

Derwent Valley is extremely popular at weekends and throughout the summer so I made sure I arrived early to guarantee a parking place at Fairholmes car park. Leaving the car park on the upper exit road, directly across from the junction I saw a track which was signed as a forest walk to Lockerbrook. The route follows this track up the hill and over a bridge where I carried on ahead, this time following directions for Lockerbrook Farm.

The path soon beared left following the Forestry Commission concessionary footpath sign. When I came to a road, I went straight across it onto the path and did the same when I came to a second road, keeping to the Lockerbrook signs. The path soon went to the right, turned back on itself and bent off to the left after passing an old ruined wall. I took the gate out of the trees onto the moor and soon after went through another gate onto a track, where I turned left. Then heading down the track, I went through another gate, passing the farm on the left. The route carried on along the track until it bent off to the right and there was a path leading off it on the right at grid reference SK 163891.

Trigs to spot from the top:

Higher Shelf Stones: 4.3km north west. **See page 71 of this book.**

Edale Moor: 5.4km south. **See page 18 of this book.**

Outer Edge: 6.1km north east. **See page 68 of this book.**

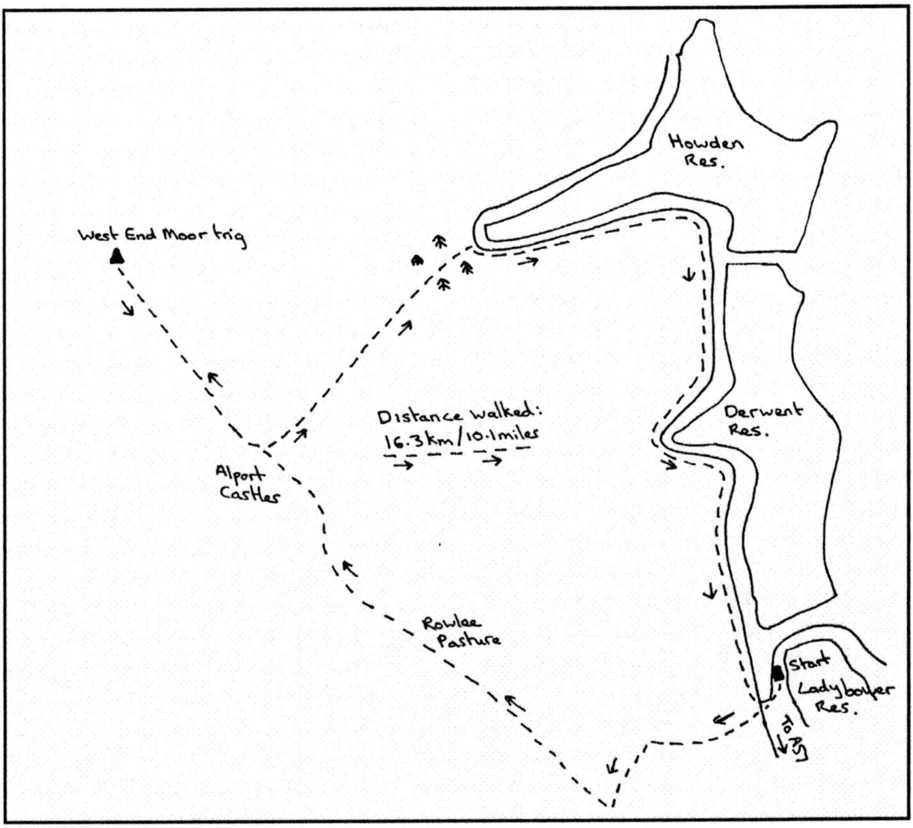

Heading up the path and going through the gate at the top of the field, I then carried on the path and cleared the stile which took me onto Rowlee Pasture. This is essentially the path to Alport Castles and the trigpoint, with the path soon turning into a man-made and easier to use surface.

When Alport Castles came into view I became aware of just how impressive a landform it is. It was not surprising to learn that it was formed by the largest inland landslip in England. On the horizon, just to the left of the Castles, is the trigpoint, for which I continued making for along the path.

Beyond Alport Castles the path went over two streams and just after the second one there was a path off to the right up the hill (SK 133927). This

path eventually levelled out at the trigpoint (S4298). I retraced my footsteps away from the trigpoint, turning left at the main path and going back over the two streams. As I arrived back at Alport Castles I looked for a large track on the left which I found opposite a broken wall at SK 141916. This track took me down to Derwent Valley and when I reached the bottom I turned right onto the track and then turned right onto the road it came out on. I followed this road past Howden Reservoir and Derwent Reservoir back to the car park at Fairholmes.

Peak District fact: In total, there are 125 parishes spread out around the National Park.

Peak District connections

Throughout this book, I've highlighted some great walks that you can plan and given tips to get the most out of the Peak District. We've also taken a look at the rock that makes up the heart of the national park and the reservoirs that provide essential supplies for those living in the area. The economy of the Peak District is reliant on tourism, this being the case because of the huge population that surrounds the park. The population that provides money for the Peak District also relies on the Peak District for the water they get through their taps. And the rocks that attract the visitors are the same ones that dam up the reservoirs and now provide tourist attractions. Man and Nature are reliant on each other in the Peak District.

Walk 18: West Nab

A short walk on Meltham Moor, though steep and rocky.

Trig Point	West Nab at 500m/1640ft (SE 076088)	
Map	LR110, EOL1	
Distance	✪✪✪✪✪	2.8km/1.75miles
Time	✪✪✪✪✪	1hr
Ascent	✪✪✪✪✪	80m/264ft
Difficulty	✪✪✪✪✪	Boggy ground after rainfall
Start and Finish	Car park on local road off A635 (SE 077076)	

ROUTE For this one, I parked in the car park, which I found on the right hand side shortly after turning off the A635 and heading on a local road towards Meltham. Walking from the car park to the road and turning right onto it, I began walking up the slope. I stuck to the road for around three quarters of a mile until I saw a concessionary footpath off to the left. Rocks were to be found at the top of the hill marking where the trigpoint lay. I made my way up the hill on the path, climbing over a stile on the way and then following wooden posts which mark the way. The trigpoint (S1756) is located at grid reference SE 076088. After enjoying the views from the top, I turned and went back down the hill, turning right at the road. Walking back down the hill to the starting point, I found the original car park on the left.

Trigs to spot from the top:

Lingards Wood: 3.3km north.

Holme Moss: 4.1km south. **See page 80 of this book.**

Wolfstones Heights: 4.8km east.

This is one of the shortest walks in the book and one of the few to be found in the northern reaches of the Peak District. As such, walkers may want to combine the venture with the Holme Moss trigpoint on Black Hill. The map below shows the routes to both trigs, which have a joint distance of around 5.5 miles.

** The map below is also for walk 20 to Black Hill.*

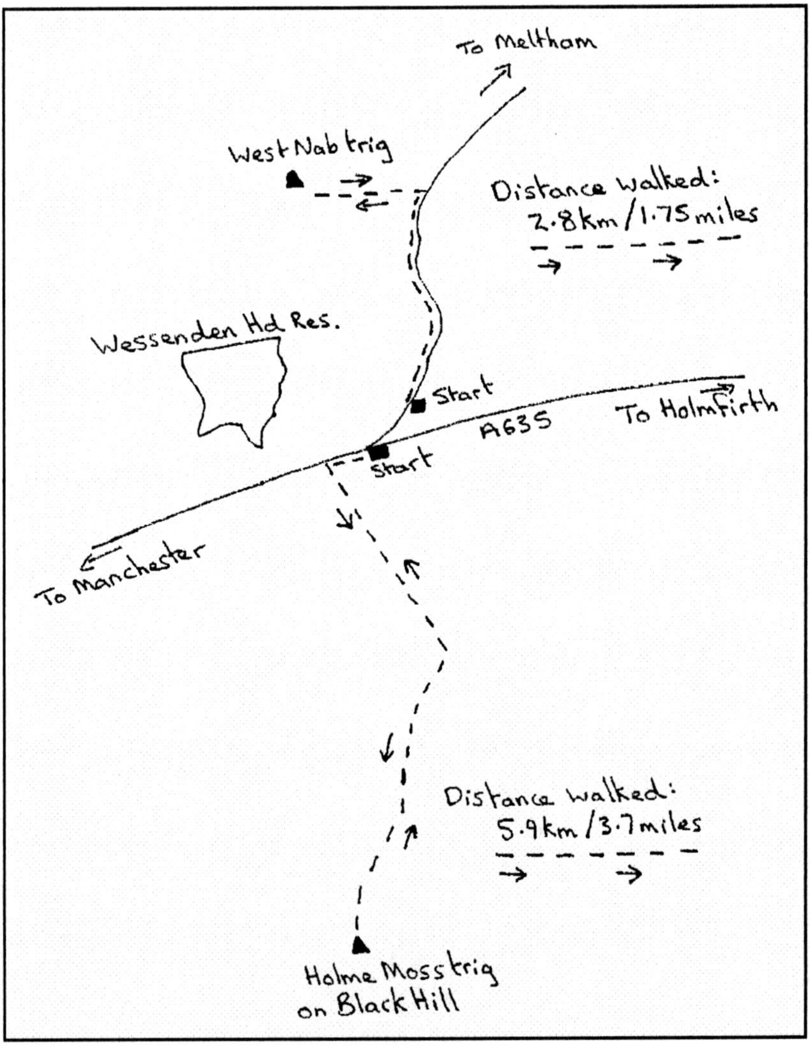

Walk 19: South Nab

A walk along the moors between Sheffield and Manchester on the Woodhead Pass

Trig Point	South Nab at 461m/1512ft (SE 156003)	
Map	LR110,EOL1	
Distance	✪✪○○○	5.6km/3.5miles
Time	✪✪○○○	1hr 10min
Ascent	✪○○○○	139m/457ft
Difficulty	✪✪○○○	Can be boggy underfoot
Start and Finish	Lay-by on A628 Woodhead Pass (SE 157001)	

ROUTE The main road between Sheffield and Manchester may seem an unlikely place to start a walk, but once away from the hum of traffic these moors can be charming. The trigpoint (S1770) does not have direct public access, but is easily visible from the road. Having parked by the road on the same side as the trig point, walkers can look at the hill that the trigpoint stands on and head left long the road towards Manchester, joining a path which runs along side a fence. I took a path which led off to the right, taking in the advice of a notice warning of boggy ground. The path wound down to Woodland Clough, bringing into sight a number of reservoirs. After crossing the stream via a bridge, a signpost sent me off to the left, with this path taking me to the

Trigs to spot from the top:

Dead Edge End: 3.5km north west.

Snailsden: 3.9km north west.

Outer Edge: 3.9km south east. **See page 68 of this book.**

left of Upper Windleden Reservoir, through a gate and up to the road. Turning left at the road, I joined both the Trans Pennine Trail and The Longdendale Trail.

When I reached the road junction, I carefully crossed the road and went straight ahead. The key here was to follow the Trans Pennine Trail and take good care to mind the traffic. As I went down into a dip I came to a dry stone wall where I took a path off to the left over a stile (SE 140001).

I now followed the path alongside a wall and continued straight on when the wall came to an end, shadowing a ruined wall. This path bent to the right and then to the left, passing the remains of Lady Cross and bringing the A628 into view once more. When I rejoined the road, I turned right and continued until I reached the starting point.

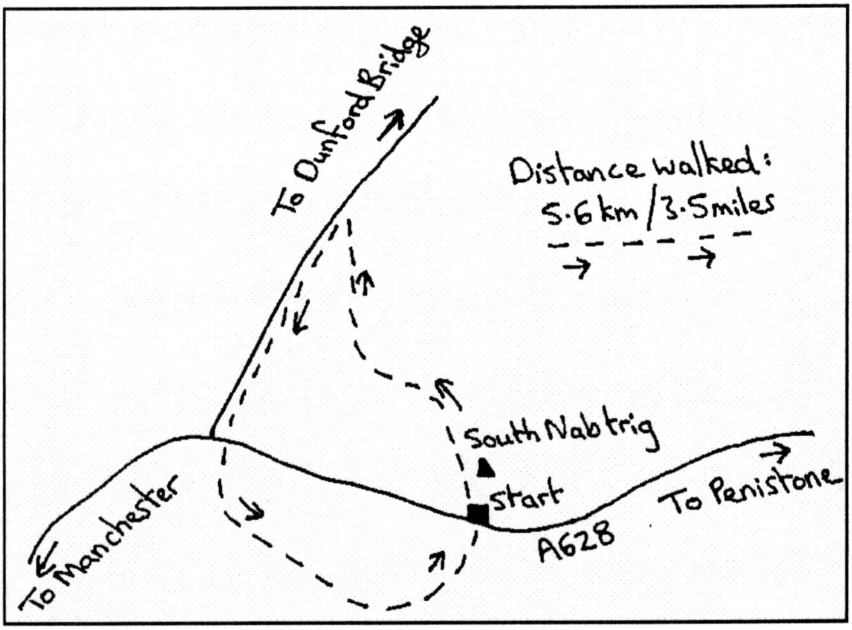

South Nab (SE 156003)

West Nab (SE 076088)

Walk 20: Holme Moss

A tough climb up to the top of Black Hill, which can be dangerous in bad weather.

Trig Point	Holme Moss at 365m/1198ft (SE 078046)	
Map	LR110, EOL1	
Distance	★★☆☆☆	5.9km/3.7miles
Time	★☆☆☆☆	1hr 40mins
Ascent	★★☆☆☆	259m/849ft
Difficulty	★★★★☆	Dangerous streams after rain
Start and Finish	Park on A635 near Meltham turning (SE 076072)	

ROUTE This walk can be highly dependent on the weather, with heavy rain making for boggy walking and some fast-flowing streams to cross. Things have been made much easier, however, by the recent building of a path to the summit. Walkers can park on the A635, from where they will need to walk west along the road towards Manchester for a short distance until seeing a footpath on the left signed for the Pennine Way. I climbed over this stile and joined the man-made path, which forms the route all the way to the trig on Black Hill. The path took me down into a small valley and over two streams before climbing up again and eventually back down into Dean Clough.

Trigs to spot from the top:

Upper Heyden: 2.1km south west.

West Nab: 4.1km north. **See page 75 of this book.**

Hey Edge: 4.6km south.

This river crossing can be problematic after heavy rain, so I was sure to be extremely careful.

The path continued on up the hill, passing a couple of cairns and eventually entering a small plateau. I crossed this until the ground became peat-based, when I again picked up the man-made path. Try to imagine what it was like getting to this trig point in the days before the path was completed! From here it is not far to the trigpoint (2958), which was on the right of the path at SE 078046. From the top I could see Holme Moss television mast to the south east. After reaching the peak, I retraced my steps down the path to the main road and start point.

** For the Black Hill map, please see the map for walk 18.*

Holme Moss (SE 078046)

My Trigpoint Notes…

Printed in the United Kingdom
by Lightning Source UK Ltd.
118383UK00002B/334-357

9 781846 854378